STAMPING
FOR FUN!

by Pamela Dell

Content Adviser: Michelle Servinskas, Owner, Stamping Cottage, Williston Park, New York
Reading Adviser: Frances J. Bonacci, Ed.D., Reading Specialist, Cambridge, Massachusetts

Compass Point Books ◆ Minneapolis, Minnesota

Compass Point Books
151 Good Counsel Drive
P.O. Box 669
Mankato, MN 56002-0669

This book was manufactured with paper containing
at least 10 percent post-consumer waste.

Photographs ©: Karon Dubke/Capstone Press, cover (all), back cover, 4–5 (all), 8, 10, 11, 12–13, 14–15 (all), 18,
19, 20, 22–23 (all), 24, 28–29, 33, 34–35, 37, 47; Enigma/Alamy, 6; Musee Dentaire, Lyon, France/Archives Charmet/
The Bridgeman Art Library, 7; Luis Castro/Shutterstock, 9; Jaimie Duplass/BigStockPhoto, 16 (top); Elizabeth Whiting &
Associates/Alamy, 16 (bottom); Feng Yu/Shutterstock, 17 (top); Thomas M Perkins/Shutterstock, 17 (middle), 43 (bottom
right); Nicole Wright, 17 (bottom); Ben Friday/iStockphoto, 21; Greg Nicholas/iStockphoto, 25; Michelle Servinskas, 26,
27; Joyce Yaari, 31; AP Images/Marcio Jose Sanchez, 38–39; Kevin Nakagawa, 40–41 (front & back), 43 (top right); Karen
Canto, 41 (right); The Granger Collection, New York, 42 (left); Library of Congress, 42 (right); RubberStampMadness, 43
(left); Rusty Jarrett/Getty Images for NASCAR, 44; Hulton Archive/Getty Images, 45.

Acknowledgment: Thanks to Nicole Wright and Rachel Dahlquist for their help with this book.

Editor: Brenda Haugen
Page Production: The Design Lab
Photo Researcher: Eric Gohl
Art Director: LuAnn Ascheman-Adams
Creative Director: Keith Griffin
Editorial Director: Nick Healy
Managing Editor: Catherine Neitge

Library of Congress Cataloging-in-Publication Data
Dell, Pamela.
  Stamping for fun! / by Pamela Dell.
      p. cm.
  Includes index.
  ISBN 978-0-7565-3862-0 (library binding)
1. Rubber stamp printing—Juvenile literature. I. Title.
  TT867.D45 2008
  761—dc22   2008008275

Visit Compass Point Books on the Internet at www.compasspointbooks.com
or e-mail your request to custserv@compasspointbooks.com

Table of Contents

Note: In this book, there are two kinds of vocabulary words. Stamping Words to Know are words specific to stamping. They are defined on page 46. Other Words to Know are helpful words that are not related only to stamping. They are defined on page 47.

Make Your Mark!

Are you ready to have fun in a creative way? All it takes is a few rubber stamps and a bit of ink. With these basic tools, you're ready to start exploring the world of rubber-stamping. Create your own one-of-a-kind greeting cards. Hang awesome art that you've created on your bedroom walls. Give your scrapbook pages some added

pizzazz. With rubber stamps, you can decorate picture frames, lampshades, clothes, and a lot more. You can even rubber-stamp cookies and other food!

Rubber-stamping is a craft limited only by your imagination. In this book you'll find lots of techniques and projects to get you started. You'll be amazed at how much you can do. Just let your creativity run wild!

Special Supplies

Not all rubber stamps are safe for stamping on food. You also need special food coloring rather than ink. Regular food coloring has too much sugar and will ruin an ink pad.

From Practical to Playful

Stamps and seals of different kinds have been used for thousands of years. But rubber stamps are a fairly new invention. In 1839, inventor Charles Goodyear (right) discovered a way to "cure" rubber. His process, called vulcanization, gave rubber a firm but flexible quality that stayed the same at any temperature. After vulcanization, the ways rubber could be used were almost endless.

No one knows who invented the rubber stamp. The first rubber stamps were probably created in the 1860s. By the end of the 1800s, they were used for many purposes. Rubber stamps were used to label equipment and other goods. They also were used to stamp dates and other information on important documents.

In time people started using rubber stamps in more creative ways. But it was not until the 1970s that art stamping really began. The craft started slowly, mainly in Southern California, and spread from there. Today the art-stamping craze is global!

Yuck!

Rubber comes from the sap of rubber trees. Until Charles Goodyear invented vulcanization, rubber was a sticky, smelly substance that had few practical uses.

Thank Your Dentist

Rubber stamps got their start thanks to dentists. After the invention of vulcanization, dentists in the 1800s used vulcanizers, small pots in which they molded rubber bases for false teeth. The first high-quality rubber stamps were created in these same little pots.

Choosing the Best Ones

It's good to know what to look for when you go stamp shopping. With a few pointers in mind, you will be able to choose stamps that give crisp, clear impressions and that last a long time.

Most rubber stamps have three parts. These are the die, the cushion, and the block.

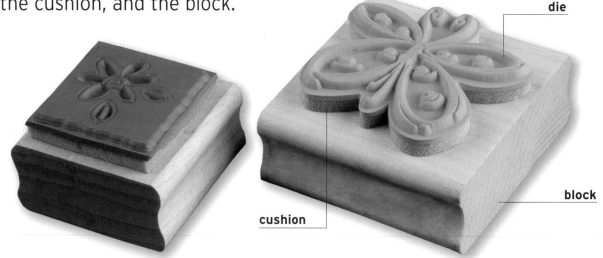

die

cushion

block

8

The die is the actual design on the stamp. Look for dies that are cut deeply into the rubber. If the die is shallow, you won't get a clear image when you stamp. Make sure the surface of the die is even, too. If it's not, some of the design will smear or won't show up at all, even if you've applied ink evenly to the whole die.

The cushion is a layer of padding usually glued between the die and the block, or handle. Look for stamps that have good cushions. If the cushion is too thin, ink may get on the edges of the rubber and leave unwanted lines when you stamp.

The block is the handle that is attached to the cushion. The block gives you something sturdy to hold on to. When you choose a stamp, select one with a block that's firm and not too big for your hand.

Block Material

Blocks are usually made of wood, but some are made from other materials, such as plastic or foam.

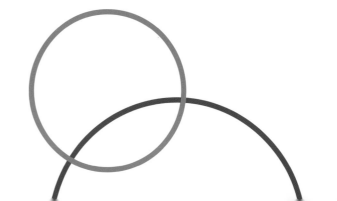

Treat Your Stamps Right

Take good care of your stamps, and they will last much longer. Keep them away from heat and direct light. It's best to put them in storage boxes when you're not using them. If they are in the sun too much, they will end up dry and cracked. It's also best to store them with the rubber side down. But the most important thing is to keep them clean. If ink builds up too much, it can eat away the adhesive, or glue, that holds the block, cushion, and die together.

Cleaning Tip #1

Sometimes bits of ink get caught in rubber stamps' crevices. To clean out this ink, wet an old, soft toothbrush, and scrub gently. You may use a tiny drop of dish soap, too, as long as it is rinsed off well. Over time some darker inks may stain the rubber, but as long as the stamps are well-cleaned, that is no problem.

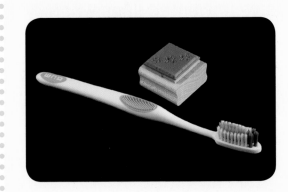

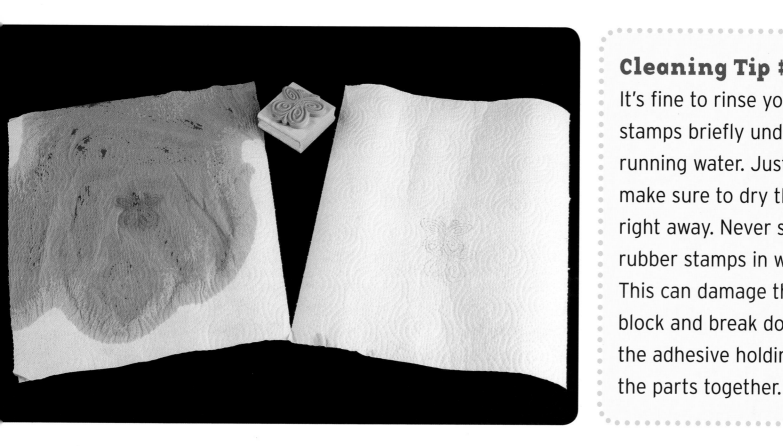

Cleaning Tip #2
It's fine to rinse your stamps briefly under running water. Just make sure to dry them right away. Never soak rubber stamps in water. This can damage the block and break down the adhesive holding the parts together.

Clean your stamps right away after each use. It's easy. Just press the stamp onto a wet paper towel. Then stamp it on a dry paper towel. Go back and forth like this until no more ink remains on the stamp. Make sure to put a piece of cardboard or a cookie sheet under the paper towels so the ink doesn't seep through to the surface beneath. And never use harsh chemicals or oil-based cleaners. They can damage the rubber.

Good Things to Know

You can't make a rubber-stamp creation without inks or paints. Store-bought ink pads are the easiest to use. Even if you use ink pads that already contain ink, you'll need re-inkers. These are containers of ink you apply to the pad once the ink is used up.

The three main types of ink are dye-based, pigment, and permanent. Dye-based inks dry quickly and create good impressions. They also tend to fade over time. Pigment inks come in richer colors and usually won't fade. They have a thicker texture, too. But watch out! Because they take awhile to dry, you risk smearing your image if you aren't patient.

Permanent inks have a lot of advantages. They dry fast, don't fade, and won't bleed into places you don't want them to. They also work well on almost any surface. The water-based varieties are best for easy use and easy cleanup.

You can buy ink pads already filled with ink, or add the ink yourself to a clean pad. Felt pads covered in linen or some other fabric are a good choice. They provide a firm surface to press your stamp on. Choose inks that are water-soluble and nontoxic. That makes them safe and easy to use. Remember to close the lids tightly when you're not using your ink pads or they will dry out.

Other Ways to Color Your Creations

Ink pads aren't your only option for coloring your work. A felt-tip marker is another great inking tool. Just apply the ink from the marker directly to the rubber stamp. If you're careful, you can experiment with applying different colors to different parts of the same stamp. You also can use colored pens to fill in parts of the image you've stamped.

Rubber-stamp artists also use paint. Some paints—such as acrylics—work well for stamping. Acrylic paints come in lots of colors, and they wash up easily if you have a spill.

You can buy bottles of different kinds of paint depending on what you need for your project.

Finally, don't forget about fabric inks and paints. These should be used when you decide to add decorative stamps to clothing or other pieces of cloth.

No matter what you use for stamping, check the directions. Some inks or paints only work well on certain surfaces. The more experience you have, the better you'll be able to predict what inks and paints will work best for any project.

Stamping Trick

Here's a trick when using markers to ink stamps. Breathe onto the inked stamp before stamping on your paper. Markers dry quickly on stamps. Your warm breath moistens the ink and helps you get a nice stamped image.

Additional Tools to Use

If you have a stamp, an ink pad, and something to stamp on, you're ready to begin. But here are a few extra tools that can help you be even more creative.

Glue: Choose glues that dry clear and have no toxic ingredients. Be sure to read the directions. Some glues only work well on certain surfaces.

Brayers: Brayers, or rollers, are made from sponge or hard or soft rubber. They are great for spreading paint or ink on stamps. You can buy brayers in home-building, craft, and paint stores. Since most stamps are not very big, you will only need small brayers.

Masking tape: Maybe you want to stamp or paint a certain area without getting ink on the rest of the paper. Mask off that part. Masking tape is great when you want straight lines in your creation, too. You also can cut paper into any shape you like and position it wherever you don't want ink or paint applied. After you're done painting or inking, remove the tape or paper cutout—and there's your shape on the page!

Scissors: You can be really creative with scissors. Sometimes you need a scissors that cuts straight lines. Other times you can be wilder and use scissors that cut zigzags or other patterns.

Stamp-placement tool: When you want to make sure your stamp is positioned exactly right, or if you need to re-stamp part of an image, this tool is important. Stamp-placement tools are usually available in craft stores. You also can find them online.

Things to Think About

You don't need to spend a lot of money to get started rubber-stamping. With just a few stamps, there is no limit to the number of projects you can create. And the different stamp styles are nearly endless. That means it won't be hard to find ones you'll love using again and again.

A Stamp for Every Job

Now that people have started stamping just about every kind of surface, stamp makers are trying new ideas, too. You can find large stamps made for big projects, such as creating borders on walls and decorating furniture.

When you first shop for stamps, start slowly and choose wisely. Pick two or three simple designs that you might be able to use in many different ways. Pick stamps that you will want to use over and over and that reflect your personality.

Use common sense when deciding where to create your stamp art. You need a firm, smooth surface—without crumbs, bubbles, or bumps. Trying to stamp while sitting in bed iş not a good idea.

Use Your Imagination

When beginning to stamp, don't be afraid to experiment. Try using your inks and stamps in different ways and on different materials. Later you can get some stamps with more detailed or unusual designs and try more complicated moves.

Where to Make Your Mark

Paper is not the only option for creating stamp art. Fabric, wood, and clay make good surfaces for stamping, too.

But make your first stamp impressions on paper. It is the easiest material to work with, and there are many fun forms of paper. You can stamp in notebooks and journals, on card stock or labels. Craft stores also sell papier-mâché picture frames and boxes that make great surfaces for stamped images. You will probably come up with at least a few ideas of your own, too.

To stamp on a T-shirt or other cloth item, be sure you have inks or paints specially made for fabric. Some acrylic paints can be used on fabric and usually produce crisp, clear images. Read all the directions carefully to make sure that you use the fabric paint properly. You don't want your image to run or fade.

You also can make great stamped images on either painted or unpainted wood. Once your stamps have dried, you can keep them from chipping by coating the whole wood surface with a matte varnish. You can buy varnishes at craft stores, paint stores, or hardware stores.

Stamping on glass or ceramic surfaces is tricky. Your stamps won't stick to an object that has a very slick or shiny coating. Before stamping a glass or ceramic item, lightly sand the surface with the finest-grain sandpaper you can find. This will help your image stick.

Ceramic tiles

Homemade Stamps

There are many ways to make your own stamps. If you are careful, you can cut out a design from an eraser or cork. And here are two other ways to make your own stamps.

Sponge stamps: Using a felt pen, draw a simple design on a firm, dry sponge. Try a heart or a star, for example. Then cut the design out with scissors. The sponge will be easier to cut if you dampen it slightly. But don't get it all wet or you'll lose your design! Wait until the sponge is dry and firm again before stamping so you can get a good grip on it.

Potato stamps: Wash and dry a potato, and then cut it in half. Be sure to cut straight through the potato so the surface is not angled. Draw a simple design on the cut surface using a felt pen. Have an adult help you cut away the parts of the potato outside the design. Make sure the design sticks up enough from the surface that its outline will be clear and separate from the rest of the potato.

Fun With Fruits and Veggies

It is fun to try your luck with other fruits and vegetables, too. For instance, cut an apple in half, and coat one whole cut surface with ink or paint. You've got an apple-shaped design!

Make a Good Impression

How your design turns out will depend on what kind of stamp, ink, and surface you decide on. But here are some hints to help you make a good impression every time.

Don't press your stamp too hard into the ink pad. Just tap gently a few times on the pad. If you have to press hard to get ink on your stamp, it may be time to add more ink to the pad. The same is true with applying paint. Just roll across the stamp once or twice. Too much ink or paint on your stamp will smear your design and make a mess. And usually, very detailed stamps need less paint or ink than more simple designs do.

When you press the stamp onto the surface, don't rock or wobble it. This can smear the edge of the image or give you a fuzzy result. Use firm,

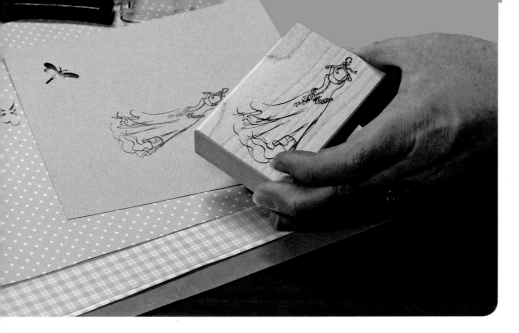

steady pressure. With larger stamps, you may need to press down harder to get crisp images. But never press really hard, or you may damage the die or cushion.

Before you work on the real thing, test out your image on some scrap paper or a piece of fabric. Then you'll see if you need more or less ink and if the whole image is showing evenly. Another trick is to stamp pieces of paper and then arrange them on the surface you plan to stamp to see how they look. If you like the design, you will feel more confident when stamping the real thing. If you don't like the way it looks, rearrange your sample stamp scraps, and try them a new way.

Getting Creative

Some stampers use a technique called stamping off to get several shades of color from a single ink pad. Stamp an image on your surface, re-ink, and then stamp a scrap paper once or twice. Finally, stamp the impression on your real creation again. You can get fun effects from using the same image more than once but with some of those images having lighter appearances than others.

Two Ways to Add Visual Interest

There are many techniques you can try once you are ready to be more creative. Here are some ways to add to your stamping fun.

Masking: This is a great way to make a stamped image look like it is behind another image. First, stamp the paper or other material you are using as your "canvas." Then stamp the same image on a sturdy piece of paper or card stock. Cut this image out, leaving only the tiniest edge around it so that this second image is slightly larger than

Masking

The stars at the bottom of this stamp-art project were created using the bleaching technique.

image is partly on the card stock and partly on the canvas itself. When you remove the card stock, the second image will appear to be behind the first one.

Bleach stamping: Choose dark-colored paper. Put a couple of paper towels into a shallow glass dish. Wearing rubber gloves, carefully pour a few drops of bleach over the paper towels. Ask an adult to help you. Don't get the towels soaking wet. Use only enough to just saturate them. Press your stamp onto the paper towel, and then press down on the colored paper. Soon the paper will begin to fade where you stamped, and a lighter-colored design will appear. Don't worry about the bleach hurting your rubber stamps. It won't. But be sure to clean the die before using the stamp with ink or some other substance.

the first one. When both stamped images are dry, place the second image on top of the first one. Ink a second stamp—or use the same one again—and stamp so that the

Greeting Cards for Any Occasion

Make a birthday card, thank you note, or any other type of greeting card you'd like.

1. Glue the background layer of paper to the card stock so that there is an even border all the way around. Smooth the paper so there are no bubbles or bumps from the glue.

2. Your card should fold at the top (horizontal card) or at the left side (vertical card). To test positioning, place the strip of card stock according to the shape of your card. Position it horizontally from edge to edge if your card folds at the top, vertically if it folds at the side.

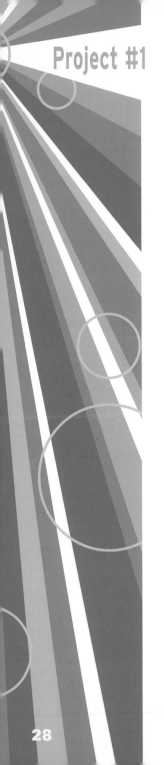

3. Before gluing the strip down, arrange felt stickers, buttons, or tiny charms on it, and glue them down. You can glue felt stickers, buttons, or charms to other parts of the card, too. Try different arrangements for your card before you glue everything in place.

4. Cut a sheet of lightweight, color-coordinated card stock into a rectangular or oval shape just big enough for your stamped impression to fit. Ink your "greeting" stamp, and stamp the smaller paper.

5. Use glue or double-sided tape to attach the stamped greeting to the card so it overlaps the strip. Open your card, and write your message inside.

Materials

- Sheet of card stock, 8 1/2 inches x 11 inches (21.6 centimeters x 28 cm), folded in half horizontally or vertically
- Background layer of paper, about 5 inches x 3 3/4 inches (12.7 cm x 9.5 cm)
- Glue stick or other clear-drying glue
- Strip of card stock, either 1 1/4 inches x 5 1/2 inches (3.2 cm x 14 cm) or 1 1/4 inches x 4 1/4 inches (3.2 cm x 10.8 cm) depending on if your card is horizontal or vertical
- Stamp that has a word, saying, or greeting, such as Happy Birthday!
- Sheet of lightweight, color-coordinated card stock
- Felt stickers, buttons, or tiny charms

Stamped Ceramic Tiles

You can come up with lots of interesting objects by stamping on ceramic tiles. Make coasters out of bigger tiles. Use small tiles to create pendants, hanging ornaments, or pins you can wear. By gluing a magnet on the back, you can make a refrigerator magnet. You can buy inexpensive tiles at home building stores.

1. Ask an adult to heat the oven to 325 degrees Fahrenheit (163 degrees Celcius).

2. Ink your stamp. Make a clear image on your tile, and let it dry.

Materials

- Ceramic tile without a design
- Stamps that will fit on the tile
- Permanent ink
- Spray matte-finish sealer, ribbon, magnet, glue (depending on your project)

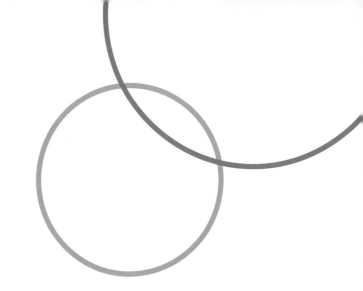

4. If, after baking, you want to color in your stamped design with ink, apply color carefully with a small brush. Then spray the design with sealer to keep it from smearing. You only need to apply sealer if you add this extra layer of color.

3. Have an adult help you put the tile directly on the oven rack, or on a baking sheet if the tile is very small. Let the tile bake for 10 to 15 minutes. This will set the ink. After the tile cools off, you're done. Don't forget to turn off the oven!

5. To make a pendant, glue a long ribbon to the back of the tile. Glue a shorter loop of ribbon to the tile for a hanging ornament. For a refrigerator magnet, glue a small magnet to the back center of the tile.

Beautiful Bookmarks

Handmade bookmarks make great gifts for others—or for yourself! With well-chosen stamps, you can create designs that reflect your style.

1. Choose a sheet of card stock, and stamp all three impressions on it. Use a different color ink for each image.

2. If you like, use markers to color in your stamped images.

3. Cut out each stamped image in a square shape, all the same size.

Materials

- Five sheets of card stock in various colors
- Three small stamps that fit a theme, such as three pet stamps, three flowers, or three cars
- Three ink colors that go well together and with the card stock
- Markers
- Scissors
- Hole punch
- Ribbon (a little wider than the hole from your hole punch)

5. Glue each stamped square to one of the colored squares.

6. Cut three squares from the fifth sheet of card stock, making them slightly bigger than the three colored squares. Glue each of the framed stamp squares to one of these larger squares.

7. Punch a hole at the top center and bottom center of each of these largest squares.

8. Cut a long piece of ribbon. Gently insert it through each hole, making sure the ribbon lies behind the squares. Leave several inches of ribbon at the top and bottom.

4. Cut one square from three of the remaining pieces of card stock. Make sure these squares are a little bigger than your stamped squares because they will "frame" the stamps.

9. Carefully tie knots at the top and bottom holes to keep the ribbon from slipping or moving. There's your bookmark!

One-of-a-Kind T-Shirt

Tips for fabric stamping:

- Experiment first on a scrap of fabric.
- Cotton or other natural fibers work best.
- Make sure your fabric is free of wrinkles.
- Work on a hard surface.
- Put cardboard inside the shirt so paints and inks don't seep through to the other side.

1. Place a piece of cardboard inside the T-shirt. Test your design on a sheet of paper before stamping. When you have made a design you like, start stamping on the front or back of your T-shirt.

2. Color in some parts of the stamps, if you like. Use pens, inks, or paints specially made for fabric.

3. When the fabric is dry, turn your shirt inside out. To set the inks, iron your shirt on the highest setting for the fabric. Don't use steam.

4. Turn your shirt right side out, and wear it proudly!

5. Wash and dry your shirt according to the label instructions.

Materials

- Cotton T-shirt
- Inks, pens, or paints that are made for fabrics
- Stamps that go well together
- Cardboard

Personalized Place Mat

Hand-stamped place mats liven up any meal. You may come up with different designs, but here's one to get you started.

1. Carefully glue the light-colored card stock to the larger, dark-colored card stock. Position the light card stock so you have a 1-inch (2.5-cm) border all around.

2. Create a border of stamped squares around the edges of the light-colored card stock. Use your border stamp and two or three ink colors that go well with the dark-colored card stock.

Materials

- Sheet of light-colored card stock, 11 inches x 14 inches (28 cm x 35.6 cm)
- Sheet of darker-colored card stock, 13 inches x 16 inches (33 cm x 40.6 cm)
- Square border stamp
- Three or four stamps small enough to fit inside the border
- Set of large alphabet stamps or individual letter stamps that spell out your name
- Several colorful ink pads
- Glue

4. Pick an ink color that goes well with your card stock colors and other stamped images. Using the letter stamps, stamp your name across the center of the light-colored card stock. If the letters are small enough to fit inside your border stamp, try stamping a square for each letter of your name. Then stamp the letters inside the squares. To change up your design, you could position your letters unevenly or stamp your name diagonally.

5. Take your place mat to an office supply store, and have it laminated—protected in a clear covering. Then you can easily wipe your place mat clean after each use!

3. Stamp an image into each square, using a random pattern of your small stamps.

Rubber-Stamping Resources

Rubber-stamp artists say the same things about one another—that stampers are creative and really friendly! This is probably because creating stamp art is so much fun. No wonder stamping is so popular.

You can join the fun, too. And it won't be any problem at all to get your supplies together. Rubber stamps come in thousands of different designs and a wide range of prices. You'll find stamps of bugs, birds, toys, plants, and people as well as sayings of all kinds. Some rubber stamps show whole scenes. Others have kooky cartoon images or simple artistic designs. Whatever you are looking for, you will probably find it!

Most craft stores sell rubber stamps. In some cities you can find specialty shops just for rubber stamps and other art-stamping supplies. These stores usually sell magazines

Craft stores often offer a wide variety of stamping paint.

devoted to rubber-stamp arts, too. These magazines show you how to do projects and let you see what other stamp artists are doing. They also contain ads for everything you might need related to stamping, including online resources.

Stamping conventions are another great resource. At conventions you can browse the booths of different companies to get lots of information and supplies.

Stamping Magazine

RubberStampMadness was the first major magazine devoted to stamp art. The first issue appeared in 1980, and it's still popular today.

The Internet also is a major resource. Hundreds of stamping Web sites offer projects and materials. You can visit the Web sites of great rubber-stamp artists around the globe, too. Who knows? You might be inspired to build your own site to show off your stamp art!

California Artists

One of the best-known stamp artists is Kevin Nakagawa (right). Raised in California, Nakagawa was making art even as a young boy. He also spent a lot of time exploring the natural beauty of California's coastline—something he still enjoys. So it is not too surprising that his specialty is creating scenic stamp designs from nature.

Nakagawa was about 9 years old when someone gave him his first set of rubber stamps. He still has those stamps and has been going strong ever since. In 1991, he graduated from college with an art degree. About two years later he started his own stamp company called Stampscapes.

Nakagawa says his job is perfect because it involves so many of his interests. "But it's not just a job," he says. "It has become a passion and a teacher of life."

One of Kevin Nakagawa's stamp-art creations

Karen Canto (below) is another California stamp artist. She has been stamping for 25 years! Before she began designing with rubber stamps, she taught kindergarten. She became interested in rubber-stamping when a friend sent her a hand-stamped greeting card. "I went berserk" for stamping, Canto says.

By 1984, Canto started her own company, Alextamping, named after her son. He was very young at the time, and some of the first stamps Canto's company made were from Alex's drawings. Canto got her husband, Carlos, interested in stamp art, too. Today they both design the rubber-stamp creations produced by Alextamping.

What Happened When?

1830   1860   1890   1920

1864–1866 The first rubber stamps are created.

1911 The International Stamp Trade Manufacturers Association forms in Chicago, Illinois.

1839 Charles Goodyear discovers a way to keep rubber solid and flexible in spite of temperature changes, a process he names "vulcanization."

1892 More than 4,000 rubber-stamp manufacturers and dealers are in business in the United States.

1975   **1980**   **1985**   **2000**   **2010**

1986 Stampa Barbara, the first store devoted just to rubber stamping, opens its doors in California.

2008 According to a Craft and Hobby Association study, more than 6.5 million households in the United States participate in rubber stamping.

1982 The first rubber-stamp convention takes place in Montrose, California, with seven companies participating. It comes to be known as the Original Rubber Stamp Convention.

2007 The Original Rubber Stamp Convention celebrates its 25th year.

1980 *RubberStampMadness*, the first widely distributed magazine for rubber-stamp art, publishes its first issue.

Fun Stamping Facts

Two early stamp makers, Louis K. Scotford and Will Day, traveled 3,000 miles (4,828 kilometers) around the American West in 1876. They took orders for stamps during the day and made them at night.

Rubber stamps belong to the manufacturing category known as "marking devices." Before rubber stamps were invented, goods were marked using stencils.

Many of the rubber-stamp companies that started in the late 1800s are still in business today.

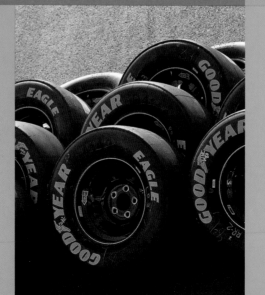

Charles Goodyear died poor, but his name was not forgotten. Goodyear is one of the leading brands of rubber tires for cars.